A VISION *for* MISSION

A VISION *for* MISSION

Daniel M. Grimwade
with
Daniel J. D. Webber and Jonathan F. Bayess

ET Perspectives No. 5

Published by Evangelical Times and
European Missionary Fellowship

Evangelical Times
Faverdale North
Darlington
DL3 0PH
England
E-mail: theeditors@evangelicaltimes.org
Web: http://www.evangelicaltimes.org

European Missionary Fellowship
Guessens, 6 Codicote Road
Welwyn
Herts.
AL6 9NB
England
Telephone: 01438 716398

First published 2010

British Library Cataloguing in Publication Data available

ISBN 10: 0-9500129-5-5
ISBN 13: 978-0-9500129-5-7

Most Bible quotations in this publication are
from the Holy Bible, New King James Version,
copyright © Thomas Nelson Inc, 1982.
Used by permission. All rights reserved.

Printed in Great Britain
by the MPG Books Group

A VISION *for* MISSION

INTRODUCTION

In his last letter to Timothy, Paul writes: 'But you have carefully followed my doctrine, manner of life, purpose, faith, longsuffering, love, perseverance' (2 Timothy 3:10). The apostle Paul clearly knew what he was trying to achieve—hence he could write, 'my purpose'.

As Paul neared the end of his life he wrote to Timothy, by now a pastor in Ephesus, to encourage him to follow his policy—that is, his blueprint for ministry and church life—which flows out of the gospel. Paul was passing on God's battle plan to Timothy, so that Timothy's ministry would have clear direction and purpose.

Twenty centuries on, the need remains pressing to have clear direction and purpose in gospel work. It is good and right to ask: 'What is the purpose of the church?' Ultimately, the aim of the church is to bring glory to God. But what must the church and its ministers do to fulfil this objective?

It is apparent from the New Testament that if the church is to glorify God, it must gather for worship and prayer, and to study God's Word. In addition, church life will be characterised by mutual love, working together, and a determination to make the gospel known.

Furthermore, this last characteristic will not be restricted to local areas but will involve efforts to see the good news preached throughout the world, in accordance with the Lord's commission (Luke 24:47; Acts 1:8). Local churches should be missionary-minded churches.

Vital work

If we are not careful, our missionary involvement will be characterised by vagueness and half-heartedness, rather than by the devotion and enthusiasm that this vital work requires.

The aim of this booklet is to help churches and ministers become mission-focused—to evaluate practically how they view mission, and how they pray for and support mission.

These chapters have been deliberately set out as Bible studies, which can be presented at midweek meetings or discussed in home groups.

Chapters 2 to 8 are a series of articles that Rev. Daniel Grimwade wrote for *ET* during 2008-2009. Chapter 1, featured in *ET* in 2009, is edited from an address given by Rev. Daniel Webber at the John Owen Centre in Finchley, London, in September 2006 at a *Mission in Europe* Conference. Chapter 9, also featured in *ET* in 2009, is edited from an address given by Rev. Dr Jonathan Bayes at the Yorkshire Reformed Ministers Fraternal, in July 2009, to mark the 500th anniversary of John Calvin's birth.

It is the prayer of the authors that this material will help churches formulate a coherent and lively missionary policy.

CHAPTER 1

REACHING EUROPEANS WITH THE GOSPEL

For more than a century, the world view of most Europeans has been shaped by a combination of philosophies, particularly relativism, pluralism and secularism.

Relativism is the view that 'true truth' (as Francis Schaeffer called absolute truth[1]) is unknowable; this is an outworking of Enlightenment philosophy. Pluralism is similar; it assumes all claims to truth are relative and therefore equally valid. It calls for universal toleration, but does not extend tolerance to those who radically disagree with pluralism.

Secularism believes that this world in its material aspect is all there is. Our stark choice is between playing the game of life—'eat, drink and be merry, for tomorrow we die' (Luke 12:19; 1 Corinthians 15:32)—or refusing to do so by means of suicide. Albert Camus, the existentialist French philosopher, argued that suicide is the 'one truly serious philosophical problem'.[2]

Spent force

Europe's peoples have also been over-exposed

to a second-hand, media-driven and usually unbiblical presentation of Christianity. This has been largely represented by images of the past derived from Christianity's history, art and architecture. These have not always been helpful representations and Christianity is now regarded as a spent force.

What about modern Protestantism? This has become woefully disconnected from its sixteenth-century roots. Theological liberalism and Barthian neo-orthodoxy have taken their toll of European theological institutions and devastated the faith and ministries of academics, pastors and church-goers. For example, 90 per cent of pastors in the Hungarian Reformed Church openly advocate a Christianity shorn of its supernaturalism.

While, interestingly enough, Calvin's *sensus divinitatis*[3] has not been eradicated from Europeans, a vacuum has been created which has been filled by Islam, Eastern and neo-pagan religions, and a quasi-religious secular humanism.

Within this context evangelicals are, uniquely, supposed to be experiencing growth. But more often their 'church growth' has come through capitulation to the thinking and behaviour of the unconverted masses. The fact is that evangelicalism too has been worn down by the effects of Enlightenment philosophy, Higher Criticism, Darwinian optimism, modern psychology and existentialism.

Pragmatic considerations

In both western and eastern Europe, many evangelical churches seem mesmerised by all that is modern. They are not so much looking to the Bible for their beliefs and practices, but to the consensus around them. The questions being asked are not 'What is true? What will God approve?', but 'What will work? What will attract the outsider?' Although theoretically the Bible is held in high esteem, pragmatic considerations often dictate the way churches think and function.

For many years, there has been a tendency to equate mission with everything Jesus expects his people to do in this world. No longer is mission seen as the church sending people to preach the gospel, in order to bring people to a saving knowledge of Jesus Christ. It is now urged to concern itself with the vast humanitarian needs of mankind, to agitate for social justice, and to work for a more ecologically-friendly environment.[4]

All these concerns are placed on the same footing as the proclamation of the gospel, but for all the good done by New Testament believers in such areas (Galatians 6:10) it is doubtful whether the apostles understood the Great Commission in this way.

While there can be no objection to individual Christians becoming involved in political, social and economic spheres, it is dangerous for churches to do so. Those churches that go this way too readily become identified with secondary issues and lesser emphases, and not with the gospel.

How is the church to respond to all this? How is she to be faithful to her missionary obligations, while being rightly sensitive to her cultural context?

Truth established

There are three priorities. First, the church must be actively engaged in establishing the truth in people's minds. We have given too much ground to the enemies of truth. Instead of being boldly set 'for the defence of the gospel' (Philippians 1:16-17), evangelicals have tended to retreat into pietistic ghettos, failing to provide 'a defence to everyone who asks you a reason for the hope that is in you' (1 Peter 3:15). Ministers and missionaries need more grounding in apologetics.

In an address delivered nearly 100 years ago at Princeton Theological Seminary, Professor J. Gresham Machen acknowledged that 'the regenerative power of God' was crucial in evangelism, yet also reminded his hearers that 'God usually exerts that [regenerative] power in connection with certain prior conditions of the human mind, and it should be ours to create, so far as we can, with the help of God, those favourable conditions for the reception of the gospel.

'False ideas are the greatest obstacles to the reception of the gospel. We may preach with all the fervour of a reformer and yet succeed only in winning a straggler here and there, if we permit the whole collective thought of the nation or of the world to be controlled by ideas which, by the resistless force of logic, prevent Christianity from being regarded as anything more than a harmless delusion'.[5]

Alongside a clear, earnest proclamation of the gospel, there must be a willingness to engage with and undermine those ideas that have reduced Christianity to the status of 'a harmless delusion'.

Light and life

Sadly, for more than a century, the emphasis in much evangelism has been placed too heavily on methodology. We have become obsessed with ways of attracting people into the churches and succeeded in doing little more than mimic the faddishness of the world. This has been closely allied to a loss of confidence in God-given truth proclaimed in the power of the Holy Spirit.

Secondly, there is a need for congregations to seek a new sense of the spiritual and eternal. The church needs life as well as light. Mission can only flourish where there is spiritual vitality among churches. It is an overspill of spiritual life.

There has been a regrettable tendency to confuse liveliness with life. Meetings have been multiplied, countless innovations adopted. But the underlying conviction seems to be that all that is needed to halt the decline is to 'tweak' the system. Interestingly, the one meeting overlooked by this approach has been 'the prayer meeting'—the place we are reminded that our sufficiency is only in God (2 Corinthians 2:16; 3:5).

The underlying problem in all of this is an absence of a sense of the greatness of God, the glory of the person and work of the Lord Jesus Christ, and the eternal destiny of all human beings.

Preachers

This absence is, in turn, related to the role and work of preachers. We are in need of *preachers* of the Word of God. We do not need mere 'talkers'; we need those who are called and gifted by God to proclaim the great truths of the gospel, in such a way that those who hear its message cannot remain immune to its claims.

The gospel needs to be preached in the power of the Holy Spirit. Its truths need to grip the lives of the people of God and, through their response to it, the lives of people outside the worshipping community. We must realise again our utter helplessness; without the intervention and aid of the living God, we can do nothing.

The resurgence of interest in Reformed theology among evangelicals over the last 50 years has brought welcome intellectual vigour and doctrinal clarity. Nevertheless, the Reformed movement must not degenerate into mere intellectualism. Nor must it forget the vital biblical distinction between primary and secondary truths. All truth is important, but not all truth is equally important.

Thirdly, the church needs to recapture a biblical view of her role in the world. Her primary task is the proclamation of the gospel. This is what she should be known for at home and overseas. In a materialistic age she must be constantly proclaiming, especially in Europe: 'For what profit is it to a man if he gains the whole world, and loses his own soul? Or what will a man give in exchange for his soul?' (Matthew 16:26).

Notes:

1. F. Schaeffer, *The God Who Is There, Complete Works*, vol. 1, Crossway, 1982, p.143.
2. A. Camus, *The Myth of Sisyphus*, Harmondsworth: Penguin, 1955, p.12.
3. J. Calvin, *The Institutes of the Christian Religion*, vol. 1, Philadelphia: Westminster Press, pp.43-47.
4. Kirk, *New Dictionary of Theology*, pp.434-436.
5. J. G. Machen, 'Christianity and Culture' from *Selected Shorter Writings* (edited by D. G. Hart), Phillipsburg: Presbyterian and Reformed, 2004, p.404.

CHAPTER 2

GOD IS A
MISSIONARY GOD

The true author of all missionary activity is the Triune God. He has always been more concerned about this work than we could ever be. Therefore, mission work should be seen, first and foremost, as his work not ours.

Mission in the Old Testament

This is the Bible's message from its opening chapters ('The Lord God called to Adam ... "Where are you?"') to its closing paragraphs ('the Spirit and the bride say, "Come!" ... And let him who is thirsty come... take of the water of life freely'). For example:

In Genesis, the Lord made the world because he is a missionary God! Although he was sufficient in himself, he chose to create a world inhabited by people so that he might relate to intelligent and sentient beings outside of himself (Genesis 1:1, 26).

When man rebelled, God promised a Redeemer (Genesis 3:15) and set out the purpose of his mission, namely, to redeem a fallen race in Christ. In Genesis 12 God called Abram through whom he intended to bless all the nations of the world—and revealed in Abraham a work of grace through faith encompassing every age and dispensation in history.

In Exodus we see the continuing purpose of God to have his own people who, despite their rebellion and disobedience, embodied the principle of free redemption and pictured the true church, 'the Israel of God' (Galatians 6:16).

In the Prophets (e.g., Isaiah 2:2-3) we see the Lord's concern for the whole world. Isaiah 9:1-2 speaks of a light shining amongst Gentiles to dispel sin and rebellion. Joel 2:32 asserts that '*whoever* calls on the name of the Lord shall be saved'—witness Jonah's commission to preach salvation to Gentile Nineveh, and the Lord's declaration in Malachi 1:11: 'my name shall be great among the Gentiles ... [and] among the nations'.

The Psalms also contain many references to the international scope of the gospel (e.g., Psalm 2:7-8; 65:2; 67:2; 102:21-22).

The Old Testament thus teaches that all mankind belongs to God and that he is concerned for their evangelisation. This is more explicit in the New Testament, perhaps, but the foundation is solidly laid in the Old. Long before the Messiah appeared on the stage of human history, God had plans and intentions for mission to all nations.

It follows, therefore, that *everything depends on the initiative of God.* Even the Old Testament's preoccupation with one nation testified to God's intention to bring the message of salvation to the whole world *through* that nation!

Mission in the New Testament

From its outset, the New Testament declares and exemplifies the worldwide character of Christ's mission and ministry:

In the Gospels: Matthew announces a Saviour who has Gentile women in his family tree; is worshipped by foreign kings; preaches first in Galilee of the Gentiles; asserts that this 'gospel of the kingdom must be preached to all nations' (24:14); and concludes by giving a glorious worldwide commission (28:19-20). And remember that in the middle of this gospel Christ says, 'I will build my church' (16:18). This is God's work and we labour as his workmen.

In Acts it is Jesus Christ himself who continues to work through his apostles. The whole book is about mission expanding in its scope (1:8). Edmond Clowney writes: 'It seems almost incredible that with the book of Acts in the Scriptures the church should ever have lost sight of its mission'. We see God fulfilling the promise of Acts 1:8 and over-ruling man's plans, for example, in Acts 16.

The Epistles echo the theme that God is a God of mission: 'And how shall they believe in him of whom they have not heard? And how shall they hear without a preacher? And how shall they preach unless they are sent?' (Romans 10:14-15; see also Colossians 1:6; 1 Timothy 2:4; 2 Peter 3:9).

Ultimately, we are left with a great vision of the success of God's missionary endeavours throughout the ages: 'I looked, and behold, a great multitude which no one could number, of all nations, tribes, peoples, and tongues, standing before the throne and before the Lamb, clothed in white robes ...' (Revelation 7:9). God is both the author and finisher of mission!

The implications for us

We see then, firstly, that *mission work is important.* How can we say we are not interested in mission when the Triune God so clearly *is*? Mission is God's work; he is doing it and wants it done.

He is the greatest missionary there ever was, sending his own Son into the world to seek and save the lost. He willingly paid the greatest possible missionary sacrifice, giving his own Son to die so that others could be saved.

If we say we love God and want to worship him, this will inevitably involve us in the work of mission. How involved we are in that work will reflect our spiritual vitality—how well we know the God of mission. As David Livingstone said, 'God had an only Son and he made him a missionary'. As we grow in grace and become more like Jesus, we will also become more concerned about world mission.

Secondly, *God determines the principles and practices of mission.* If the living God stands behind all missionary endeavour, then it is for him to decide how mission should be conducted.

Incredibly, God has chosen to use us as agents in this great enterprise, but it is still his work and he must dictate its principles, priorities and practices. We are not free to do his work our way, but must rather seek to do it his way.

When we turn to the New Testament, we find there are principles set down for how we should go about the work of mission. God tells us what constitutes mission, whose responsibility it is, how it should be undertaken, what its aim is and who should be sent out. It is God's work and our directions must come from him.

Thirdly, *the missionary task will be successful.* Our greatest encouragement to persevere in the work of mission comes from the fact that—just because it is God's work rather than our own—it will be crowned with success. Revelation 7:9-10 shows us that the redeemed from every tribe, nation and tongue will most surely be *there* in heaven. The elect will be gathered in and nothing will thwart God's plans and purposes.

Our God is a missionary God, and so mission is important. It is a most amazing thing that he privileges us to be involved. May he give us a renewed desire to see the good news of Jesus Christ proclaimed to the very ends of the earth.

CHAPTER 3

CONSCIOUS FAITH IN JESUS CHRIST IS ESSENTIAL FOR SALVATION

In chapter 2 we saw that 'God is a missionary God'. This is the first and fundamental idea we must grasp if we want to establish biblical principles of mission and ensure that our practice as churches has clear purpose and direction.

We saw that the Bible reveals God's purpose to 'save that which was lost' (Matthew 18:11) and noted three implications: (a) Mission work is important; (b) God determines the principles and practices of mission; and (c) the missionary task will be successful.

Having established that God does save the lost, and that he is the author of mission, we must next be clear on *how* God saves sinners. The answer will shape our missionary endeavour, defining what is necessary for the task.

One of the best-known verses in the Bible tells us how God saves: 'For God so loved the world that he gave his only begotten Son, that whoever believes in him should not perish but have everlasting life' (John 3:16).

He saves sinners through the work of his Son, Jesus Christ, in whom people must believe.

To believe they must hear, and if they are to hear someone must preach (Romans 10:14).

Conscious faith in Jesus Christ is essential for salvation

The plain and simple message of the New Testament is that God has provided a wonderful salvation for sinners through Jesus Christ, and whoever believes in him will receive it (John 3:15, 16, 36; 20:30-31; Acts 16:30-31; Romans 3:21-22; 10:13-15; Ephesians 2:8).

The aim of all missionary work, then, is to bring about 'obedience to the faith among all nations for his name' (Romans 1:5). Scripture is clear that Jesus is the only Saviour and that faith in him is necessary for salvation.

This doctrine is being questioned today in three ways that have serious implications for the work of mission:

1. Will anyone experience eternal conscious torment under God's wrath?
2. Is the work of Christ necessary?
3. Is conscious faith in Christ necessary for salvation?

As John Piper says: 'Biblical answers to these questions are crucial because in each case a negative answer would seem to cut a nerve of urgency in the missionary cause ... There is a felt difference in the urgency when one believes that hearing the gospel is the only hope that anyone has of escaping the penalty of sin and living forever in happiness to the glory of God's grace'.

So how does Scripture reply to these challenges?

Will anyone go to hell?

Many who see Christ as humanity's only hope, nevertheless deny that there is eternal punishment for not believing in him. Some say all will eventually be in heaven; others dismiss eternal punishment because they think the fires of hell annihilate those who reject Christ—unbelievers simply cease to exist and experience no conscious, everlasting punishment.

This, of course, has a direct bearing on the work of mission, because it affects how seriously we treat it. Is eternal punishment at stake or do unbelievers just face nothingness? What does Christ save people *from*?

The Bible's answer is that 'salvation' means 'deliverance from the eternal punishment of sin'. In this chapter we can only deal with the matter briefly, but just listen to the words of Jesus as he spoke on several different occasions: Matthew 13:49-50; 18:8-9; 22:13; 25:41, 46; Mark 9:43, 47-48.

Look also at the picture painted for us in Revelation 15 and 21:8. This is not about what 'makes sense' to us, or what is popularly believed or cleverly taught today—it is about what the glorious God has inalterably declared in his Word. He determines what is real. People's lives hang by a thread over an endless hell—as a just, fair judgement upon sin.

But God in grace has provided a Saviour.

Is the work of Christ necessary?

Many today deny that Christ is humanity's only hope. They acknowledge the work of Christ as useful for Christians but not necessary for non-Christians. The question may be put like this: 'Is the work of Christ the only means provided by God for the eternal salvation of all types of people?' or are there other bases on which the 'lost' can be sought and saved?

The Bible is emphatic that Jesus Christ, in his work and person, is absolutely necessary for salvation. There simply is no other way, truth or life, for no one can come to the Father except through him (John 14:6).

Christ's work is unique, and he has done everything needed to provide salvation from sin. For example, Romans 5:17-21 shows the universal scope and unique saving capacity of Christ's work.

Other passages, such as Acts 4:12, 1 Timothy 2:5-6 and Revelation 5:9-10, insist upon this. This is the very foundation of mission according to Jesus himself (Luke 24:46-47).

Is conscious faith in Christ essential?

Some don't deny hell or the necessity of Christ's work, but rather question whether a person's faith in Christ must be conscious. They suggest it might be possible never to hear of Jesus, but still be saved by him—it is possible to be a 'pagan saint'! One advocate of this view is Peter Cotterell, the former principal of London Bible College and author of *Mission and Meaninglessness.*

Such theories are not new, and the Bible is very clear in its response (e.g., in Romans 10:12-18). The necessity of conscious faith in Christ was Paul's conviction and it underpinned his own missionary labours (Acts 26:15-18).

Cornelius (Acts 10:1-43) is often cited as an example of a man who was 'saved' before he heard about Jesus (10:1-2, 35). But Acts 10:43 and 11:13-14 explain what Cornelius' position really was.

God does indeed honour those who seek him—but he does so by sending gospel preachers to proclaim to them the person and work of Jesus Christ! Why did God bother to send Peter to Cornelius and his household if they didn't need the *explicit* gospel message to believe and be saved?

The undeniably biblical principal is that conscious faith in the person and work of Jesus Christ is necessary for anyone to be saved from hell and to gain heaven.

The implications for us

What, then, are the implications of this for us today?

Firstly, ***the need for gospel missionary work is real***. People will perish in their sins and go to a lost, tormented eternity if they have not 'believed in the name of the only begotten Son of God' (John 3:18).

The message of Jesus Christ is the only truly good news for sinners and the Lord has given us—his church—the responsibility to take it to the 'unreached' world. We must engage with the Lord of glory in his cause.

Charles Hodge was right to declare that 'the solemn question, implied in the language of the apostle, "how can they believe without a preacher?", should sound day and night in the ears of the churches'.

The modern abandonment of this belief—the universal necessity of hearing the gospel for salvation—cuts a nerve in missionary motivation. It waters down the Great Commission. Those who carry the gospel message have beautiful feet because they 'preach ... the unsearchable riches of Christ' (Ephesians 3:8), without which no one will be saved!

Secondly, *the church's mission is to evangelise*, that is, to bring the gospel of Jesus Christ to the lost. We must never lose sight of the fact that conscious faith in Jesus is necessary for salvation. And if that is so, the church's primary concern must be to preach the gospel message knowing that 'faith comes by hearing, and hearing by the word of God' (Romans 10:17). We must keep focused on the task.

Today, a much broader definition of the church's mission is generally accepted, including—and giving the same level of priority to—stewarding the material resources of creation, practising humanitarianism and promoting social justice.

These matters are not unimportant, and Christians have responsibilities in such areas, but they are not the primary mission of the church of Jesus Christ. People need the gospel more than anything else—that must always be the number-one issue for the church.

Thirdly, *we have the privilege of being involved in God's great purpose.* It is our unspeakable privilege to be caught up with God in the greatest movement in history—the ingathering of the elect from 'all nations, tribes, peoples and tongues' (Revelation 7:9). This engagement will last until the full number of the Gentiles comes in, all Israel is saved, and the Son of Man descends with power and great glory as King of kings and Lord of lords.

God has chosen to save the lost through faith in his Son, so that in the end there will be a great multitude who worship him through Jesus Christ for all eternity. We must do all we can to declare him to the whole world.

CHAPTER 4

TO REACH
ALL NATIONS

A ny thinking about mission must begin with the fact that *God is a missionary God* and he is the author, definer and finisher of mission. The way that God has chosen to save sinners from the hell they deserve is by faith in the person and work of the Saviour of sinners. The normal way God brings people to faith in Christ is through hearing the good news of the gospel from someone who is already a believer.

Therefore, those of us who have believed have a responsibility to pass on the message to those who have not heard. But, when thinking about the task of mission, is our only concern to reach individuals with the gospel? Is mission just about winning as many as possible to Christ in other places? The answer to this is no.

What is the purpose of mission?

The promise of Christ in Acts 1:8 is that the witness will extend to the ends of the earth. So how do we know where to go when there are people perishing everywhere? What right do we have to send people to other countries with different needs when there are still great needs at home?

God's way of ensuring that all whom he wants to save hear the good news is to give us a strategy for mission which is not haphazard. He has given us the task of taking the gospel to every nation, to every people-group of the world.

The Great Commission

Our commission is to reach *nations* and not just people. How can we be sure that this is the case? Is it biblical to define the missionary task as the reaching of all the unreached peoples of the world? We are using the word 'peoples' here with the sense of 'people-groups'—those sharing ethnicity, culture and language. There is considerable biblical evidence that this is the case.

In the Great Commission the Lord Jesus Christ clearly addresses not just the apostles themselves but the whole church in all ages (Matthew 28:18-20; Luke 24:45-49; Acts 1:8). Notice the phrase Jesus uses: 'all nations'.

What did he mean by this? Did he mean 'all individual Gentiles' (as in Matthew 25:32) or 'all people-groups' (as in Acts 17:26)?

The Greek word for 'nation' is *ethnos*, from which we get words like 'ethnic'. It means a race or tribe, especially a non-Jewish one. The singular form never refers to an individual person, but always to a tribe or people-group (Matthew 24:7;

Acts 2:5; 1 Peter 2:9; Revelation 5:9). It is difficult to be dogmatic on the basis of words alone, but it seems to be steering us towards interpreting the Great Commission in terms of 'all people-groups'.

The Gentiles must hear

In the Old Testament we find God's promises to Abraham (Genesis 12:1-3; 22:18). The first promise refers to 'all the families', meaning tribes or clans, small groupings of people. The repeated promise refers to 'all the nations' in the same context.

The consistent idea is of the gospel reaching every people-group, rather than just random anonymous individuals. This same emphasis is to be found in many other Old Testament prophecies (Psalm 22:27-28; 67:1-5; Isaiah 52:10). The promised blessings are for the nations.

Paul's view of the missionary task in Romans 15:8-24 is that following the coming of Christ the Gentile nations must now hear the message. He quotes a series of Old Testament passages, which, taken together, clearly focus on people-groups. This focus governed Paul's missionary practice.

In verse 19 Paul says he has 'fully preached the gospel of Christ' and in verse 23 he goes on to say that there is no room for him to work any longer in those areas. What does he mean? That everyone in the whole region had been converted?

Clearly, that was not the case. Paul's view of his task as a missionary was not simply to win more people to Christ but to win more and more *peoples*, or nations. He was gripped by a vision of reaching previously unreached people-groups. That was why he wanted to go to Spain—to preach to peoples there who had not yet heard (vv. 20-21). Paul's calling was to be a pioneer missionary.

John's vision in Revelation 5:9-10 gives us a view of the climactic outcome of the task of mission—there will be one church gathered together into heaven from every people-group in the world.

These things should also be true of us. Our missionary focus, and our commission from the Lord, is to reach nations with the gospel.

Implications for the church

First of all, *we need to take our domestic evangelistic responsibilities seriously*. Our nation was once an unreached people-group but, in his mercy, God sent men to preach the message of the kingdom here. Now that the church is established in our nation, we have the responsibility of maintaining that witness within our own culture.

Thus, having left Timothy to pastor the church in Ephesus, Paul instructs him to 'do the work of an evangelist' (2 Timothy 4:5). Paul expects the local churches he has planted to go on with the work of evangelism (1 Corinthians 3:6-10).

The model that flows from this principle is this: pioneer missionaries plant a church among an indigenous people, who then continue to witness to their own people, while the pioneer missionaries move on to continue breaking new ground.

Secondly, *the world still needs both types of missionary*—those like Paul and those like Timothy. Timothy had left his home (Lystra, Acts 16:1), joined a missionary team, crossed cultural boundaries and then remained to oversee the newly planted church in Ephesus (1 Timothy 1:3).

Far from his homeland, Timothy stayed to minister on the mission field long after the church planted there had its own elders (Acts 20:17). He was engaging in the second part of the Great Commission—'teaching them to observe all things that I have commanded you'. With our strong heritage of theology and literature, we also have an essential role to play in carrying out this command. We can and should be providing books and theological training to those without this background.

Paul, on the other hand, was driven by a passion to make Christ known among all the unreached people-groups (UPGs) of the world. He was engaging in the first part of the Great Commission—'Go and make disciples of all nations'. If we are to be faithful to this command of the Lord, we need to have an interest in Paul-type missionaries as well as Timothy-type missionaries.

We can complete the work

There are still some 6,000 UPGs. For example, in the region of Bihar Jharkhand in North India there is a population of 75 million and 80 UPGs. According to Operation China there are 574 UPGs in China.

The Buriat people, numbering about 65,000, live in China but also overlap into Mongolia and Russia. In terms of their religion, they are shamanists with no known believers among them. These are just examples and for every one of those 6,000 people-groups there is a similar story.

One possibly unexpected result of this understanding of the Great Commission is that *the task is capable of being completed*. The population of the world doubled between 1970 and 2000. With statistics like that, it is easy to feel that it is impossible to reach everyone. But, in fact, the number of *people-groups* remains constant at around 12,000.

The task of taking the gospel to all the nations of the earth is not beyond the church of Jesus Christ. Matthew 24:14 tells us that the gospel *will* be preached in the whole world and to all nations prior to Christ's return.

That does not mean it will be easy. It will require an army of missionary families many hundreds of thousands strong. It will need gifted, trained, dedicated and determined ambassadors to win all these UPGs for Christ. In many countries there is fierce resistance to missionaries having access to UPGs at all, and missionaries have to work in secret and in constant danger of their work being stopped.

If we are to carry out the Lord's commands to evangelise the world, we will need to be radical. To ignore the cause of mission would be the same as to deny our Saviour, who said, 'As the Father has sent me, I also send you' (John 20:21). We need to have a world mission orientation and to be engaged in this work.

God's people must pray, and each church should adopt a UPG and pray for a church to be established there. The Lord has promised success. We live in exciting times!

CHAPTER 5

THE LOCAL CHURCH—GOD'S AGENT FOR MISSION

The task of mission is a great one and we all need to understand it—in order to be focused and responsible in the way we encourage or take part in it. We need biblical principles to guide us.

So far we have set out three principles which build on one another. First, the fact that God is a missionary God is the great foundation on which everything else rests. Then the way God has chosen to save people is through conscious faith in his Son. Finally, in order to have this faith people must hear the gospel of truth—which is why missionaries are needed.

God has commissioned us to reach nations with the gospel, and to ensure that God's purpose will be realised—of drawing to himself those from every tribe, tongue, nation and people.

But now we need to define who God has made responsible for this great missionary task. Until now, we have spoken of 'we' and 'us'—but who is this? Christians in general, mission societies or local churches?

The local church

God has no need to use 'means' in the work of evangelising the world. That is to say, he could, if he chose, speak directly to people to tell them the gospel himself. However, usually, God does use means—people like us, Christians who have heard the gospel, believed it, put their faith in Jesus Christ and who then go on to tell the gospel to others.

God has laid the responsibility of mission on his people, and specifically on the local church, the body of Christ.

In the Great Commission (Matthew 28:18-20) Jesus gives his disciples this mammoth task of reaching all the nations of the world. How are they going to do it? The model is set down for us in the book of Acts.

Everything in place

The book of Acts opens with a reminder that this is the ongoing work of Christ (1:1), and before Jesus ascends into heaven he confirms what he wants his disciples to do (1:8).

The book divides into three sections—the work in Jerusalem (chs. 1-7), the work in Samaria (ch. 8) and the conversion of the Gentiles (ch. 9 onwards). After Paul's conversion (ch. 9) Peter is taught that the gospel is for Gentiles as well as the Jews (ch. 10) and he reports back to the church in Jerusalem (ch. 11).

Most of the believers in Jerusalem are scattered by persecution, and as a result the gospel reaches Antioch. A great number of Gentiles are converted and a church is planted there (11:19-30). Paul is brought in to teach them and, for the first time, disciples are called 'Christians'.

Now everything is in place to begin in earnest the missionary outreach to the nations of the world. A series of churches has been established from Jerusalem to Antioch, each bringing the gospel to its region and spreading the message onward into unreached territory. All the apostles have grasped that the gospel is for Gentiles too, and Paul—Christ's chosen ambassador to the Gentiles—has been converted.

The Holy Spirit calls the local church in Antioch to set apart Paul and Barnabas for the mission field (13:1-3). Jesus' concern for the 'Lord of the harvest to send out labourers into his harvest' (Matthew 9:38) is beginning to bear fruit.

Sending body

Thus, by the Holy Spirit's command, the local church at Antioch becomes the sending body. The missionary activity is not directed by the apostles from their base in Jerusalem, but by the local church in Antioch. The same pattern is repeated later with Timothy (Acts 16:3; 1 Timothy 4:14). There is no hierarchy from the Jerusalem church downward, and the responsibility of the local church in Antioch does not end with sending individuals to the task.

The local church continues to have a duty of care towards those sent out. In Acts 14:26-28 Paul and Barnabas are seen reporting back to the church in Antioch. As churches are established they become involved in the great missionary task by means of prayer and financial support (Philippians 4:14-18; Colossians 4:2-4; 3 John 5-8; Romans 15:28-32). Even in troubled churches, believers like Gaius (3 John) are encouraged to care for passing missionaries, despite the strife in the local church.

The pattern set out for us, therefore, is one in which local churches send out members they have recognised as gifted by the Holy Spirit to preach the gospel—supporting them materially and in prayer, recognising churches established in other places as their brethren, and cooperating with them in the missionary task.

Thus the aim of mission is to see more churches established and biblically equipped. This is what Paul did as he went to Philippi, Corinth, Thessalonica—in each place a church was established, taught, and elders appointed to care for the flock. Many of the New Testament letters were written on the mission field to churches established by mission.

The work of mission should be church-based and church-focused at both ends. A church should do the sending of missionaries and a planted church should be the result.

Implications for our churches

What are the implications of this? First, that each local church has a part to play—certainly in bringing the gospel to its local area. But also, each church is called by God to be proactive, contributing to the task of reaching all nations with the gospel of Jesus Christ and seeing churches planted. None of us can abdicate from the Great Commission. It is ours to fulfil, as much as it was for the eleven apostles.

What can we do? All the things the Antioch church did:

We can send—missionaries come from churches. We must always be cultivating, encouraging, praying and expecting God to raise up people from our midst to be involved in his service. We need missionaries both like Paul (to plant churches) and like Timothy (to establish churches).

We can help finance those sent from other churches—as the Philippians gave to Paul. We should be putting a good proportion of our money into the cause of making Christ known across the world, consistently supporting faithful workers.

We can be involved in training, encouraging and teaching—giving placements to young men; supporting sound Bible colleges; releasing Bible teachers to help others; and corresponding with missionaries, demonstrating an interest in their work.

We can pray—Paul was always encouraging churches to pray for gospel work. Our prayer can change the world.

Cooperation

Cooperation between churches is to be expected. The New Testament pattern is of local churches which, although independent, cooperate and work together—particularly in terms of world mission.

We have to work hard at partnerships for the sake of the gospel. Working with others takes a great deal of effort and sometimes complicates matters, but it is necessary for the cause of the gospel.

This is where mission societies can be of great help—acting as facilitators and administrators for cooperation and avoiding duplication of effort. But they need to be church-minded and faithful to the biblical gospel, recognising that God's agency for mission is the local church and not the society itself.

The aim is to see new, self-supporting, missionary-minded churches established. The Pauline pattern of church-planting should be the goal of all missionary work. We want these churches to become self-supporting and then to contribute to the missionary cause themselves.

It is all too easy to create churches which are dependent, rather than independent. The norm should be for indigenous pastors to lead churches, though this may not always be the case, as was evident in the New Testament (look at Antioch's eldership, Acts 13:1).

Once a church is established we should respect and work with it—not seeing it as less significant because we helped establish it. Being church-based has effects at both ends—here in terms of sending and support, there in terms of respect and cooperation.

Integrity

Finally, we must seek to maintain the integrity of our missionary work and links. Our commitment to making the gospel known in doctrine and practice needs to be consistent with our own basis of faith.

We must not have double standards—preaching and teaching certain truths as important to us, but then supporting works and ministries which neglect or deny those truths in other places.

We need to have the same outlook as Paul—fixed, flexible and focused (1 Corinthians 9:19-27). He was fixed on gospel truth, determined to win others and bring them into obedience to Christ's law. He was flexible on everything else, and he remained focused on the task. That same biblical integrity and balance of principles should govern our missionary work and fellowship links.

Heed the call of Isaiah 54:2-3, and remember William Carey's dictum: 'Expect great things from God. Attempt great things for God!'

CHAPTER 6

WILLING TO
SUFFER FOR CHRIST

The final question we must consider is this: Who should the church send? God's agency for mission is the local church, but churches send out missionaries who are people. What type of people does the missionary cause need?

They must be sacrificial, Christ-centred people who are willing to suffer for Jesus' sake and the blessing of his people (Philippians 3:8; 2 Timothy 2:10). From this flows a model for the kind of mission which ensures that all whom God plans to save will hear the good news.

Willing to suffer

The great passion of missionary-minded people is the glory of Jesus Christ, and they will do anything he asks for the sake of his name. Consider Matthew 19:23-29—the discussion that follows Jesus' encounter with the rich young ruler—when Peter rehearses the sacrifices the disciples have made and Jesus assures them that it has been noted.

Jesus uses a key expression in verse 29: 'for my name's sake'. Here is the motive for missionary service—it is done for the sake of Jesus' name, for his reputation and glory. This follows because God's goal is that his Son's name should be exalted and honoured among all the peoples of the world.

The same phrase keeps appearing in the pages of the New Testament. In Acts 9:16 Paul is told that not only will he be God's missionary to the Gentiles for the glory of Jesus Christ but he will also suffer for the sake of that name.

When Paul, ending his third missionary journey, was warned not to go to Jerusalem, he replied that he was 'ready to die' for the name of the Lord Jesus (21:13). For Paul, the glory of Jesus' name and his Lord's reputation in the world were more important than life. That is the type of person the missionary cause needs. That is why Paul was sent out from Antioch (13:1-3; see also Romans 1:5).

Such thinking is typical of those who spread the gospel. John urges Gaius to send missionaries on their way 'in a manner worthy of God ... because they went forth for his name's sake'. He continues, 'We therefore ought to receive such, that we may become fellow workers for the truth' (3 John 6-8).

To be effective in the missionary cause, whatever your role, you need to be utterly convinced that 'the name of Jesus Christ' is altogether worthy. You must see the magnificence of Christ. We shall have no desire to draw others into our worship if we have no passion for worship ourselves.

Strong in passion

We measure the value of something by what we will gladly give to get hold of it. If we will sell everything to gain it, then its value is supreme. If not, it means we treasure more what we already have (Matthew 13:44).

If we view Christ as supreme—treasuring him above everything else—we shall be willing to suffer for his sake, and even give our lives should he ask (Hebrews 10:32; 11:23; 12:1-2). All these people in Hebrews had such joy in God that they were willing to suffer. This is the mindset which must dominate us if the nations are to be reached.

This is nothing more than Jesus asks of all his disciples (Mark 8:34-35). The attitude of self-denial is essential for the work of mission. When Jesus sent the Twelve on their first preaching mission he told them to expect suffering as part of the work they would do (Mathew 10:16-25)—and again it is all 'for [Christ's] name's sake' (v.22).

Note also that when Jesus speaks about the end of the age (Matthew 24:9-14), the two things that go hand in hand are suffering (v.9) and the proclamation of the gospel (v.14). This is the price of mission and it is going to be paid. The question is: Are we willing to be involved and pay that price if called to do so?

The usefulness of suffering

But why should God call on us to suffer? There are several reasons.

Firstly, *suffering makes others bold*. Philippians 1:14 shows how God uses the suffering of his devoted emissaries to make a sleeping church wake up and take risks for God.

For example, the execution of Wycliffe missionary Chet Bitterman by a Colombian guerrilla group in March 1981 unleashed an amazing zeal for the cause of Christ. He was killed by a single bullet to the chest. In the year following Chet's death, 'applications for overseas service with Wycliffe Bible Translators doubled. This trend was continued'.[1] This is not our way to motivate missionary activity, but sometimes it is God's!

Secondly, *suffering shows the love of Christ*. Paul seems to take the idea one step further: not only is suffering the price, but it is also the *means* God has ordained to finish the work (Colossians 1:24-26; 2 Corinthians 1:5-6).

Through our suffering, God makes a visible demonstration to the world of the sufferings of Christ. Suffering is an ordained means of reaching the peoples of the world and the hearts of the lost.

Thirdly, *suffering is often the seed-bed for missionary zeal*. The first man to die for the cause of Jesus Christ was Stephen. His suffering had an immense missionary impact (Acts 8:1; 11:19)—even before we consider the effect of his testimony on Saul of Tarsus. Without it, none of these things might have happened.

The lesson here is that comfort, ease, affluence, prosperity, safety and freedom often lead to great indolence in the church (Revelation 3:14-22). Conditions that ought to produce a creative investment of time and money for the missionary cause produce instead the exact opposite—apathy, lethargy, self-centredness and a preoccupation with security. The richer we are, the smaller the percentage of our income we give to mission and the less willing we are to give up our comforts for his name.

Implications for the church

There are lessons here for all of us. Firstly, *we need to get radical.* We cannot just ignore the cause of mission—it would be the same as denying our Saviour. After all, Jesus has sent us (John 20:21). We need to have a world mission orientation and to be engaged in this task in one way or another.

Secondly, *we need to lower our expectations for this life.* We have swallowed the philosophy that advises us to 'eat, drink and be merry, for tomorrow we die'. We put so much of our energy into this life, but the desire for riches and a comfortable lifestyle is deadly.

We need to be shaped by the economics of Christ rather than the consumer culture—to stop building bigger barns and, instead, show the world that we seek riches in heaven. The glory of Jesus' name among the nations is more important than our comfort and security now.

Thirdly, *we need to be willing to take risks*. Too often we hold back from being bold because we are unwilling to suffer. We must be willing to suffer reproach 'outside the camp' just as our Saviour did (Hebrews 13:12-14).

An aging Christian once objected to John G. Paton's plan to go as a missionary to the South Sea Islands. 'You'll be eaten by Cannibals!' he warned.

Paton responded: 'Mr Dickson, you are advanced in years now, and your own prospect is soon to be laid in the grave, there to be eaten by worms.

'I confess to you, that if I can but live and die serving and honouring the Lord Jesus, it will make no difference to me whether I am eaten by Cannibals or worms; and in the Great Day my resurrection body will arise as fair as yours in the likeness of our risen Redeemer'.[2]

How else will the nations be won? Many Muslim converts will risk their lives to follow Christ. Will we risk ours to win them?

Finally, *we need to be joyfully satisfied with Christ*. If we do not treasure him we will not be willing to suffer for the sake of his name. After lives of extraordinary hardship and loss, both Hudson Taylor and David Livingstone said, 'I never made a sacrifice'. Why? They were totally satisfied with Christ and believed that what they had in him was far greater than any losses they had borne. Do we value Christ that much?

Notes:

1. Steve Estes, *Called to Die* (Grand Rapids: Zondervan, 1986), p.252.
2. James Paton, ed., *John G. Paton: Missionary to the New Hebrides, an Autobiography* (1889, 1898; reprint, Edinburgh: Banner of Truth Trust, 1965), p.56.

CHAPTER 7

ENGAGING
WITH MISSION

In previous chapters, we have examined five principles about mission taught in Scripture. Mission begins with God, who has chosen to save sinners; conscious faith in Jesus Christ is necessary for salvation; we seek to reach nations and not just individuals; the local church has been given the responsibility for mission; and mission requires people prepared to suffer for the name of Jesus Christ. From these principles flow ten important conclusions.

Missionary work challenges our priorities.

How can we say we are not interested in mission when the God of the Bible is so clearly a God of mission? He is the greatest missionary that there ever was; he sent his own Son into the world to seek and save the lost.

Missionary work is urgent.

People are perishing in their sins and heading for a lost eternity. The only good news for them is in the message of Jesus Christ. God has given Christians the responsibility to take the gospel of Jesus Christ to an unreached world, and we must engage with the Lord of glory in his cause.

Missionary work evangelises the lost.

Conscious faith in Jesus Christ is necessary for salvation—and it is the church's primary task to preach that message. We must keep focused on that task. Other good works have their place in Christian living and witness, but people need the gospel more than anything else.

Missionary work needs both Pauls and Timothys.

Timothy left home, joined a missionary team, crossed cultures and ended up overseeing the young church in Ephesus far from his homeland. He stayed and ministered on the mission field long after the church there was planted with its own elders.

He was engaged in the second part of the Great Commission, 'teaching them to observe all things that I have commanded you'. Paul, on the other hand, was driven by a passion to make Christ's name known among the unreached people-groups of the world.

If we are to be faithful to the Great Commission we need both types of missionary.

Missionary work means church involvement.

God has chosen to use the church to accomplish his purposes. It is, therefore, our unspeakable privilege as Christians to be caught up by God in the greatest movement in history—the ingathering of the elect into the church from all nations of the world, until the full number comes in and Christ in all his splendour returns.

Missionary work means cooperation.

The New Testament pattern is that, while remaining independent, local churches will cooperate and work together, particularly for world mission. We have to work at partnerships for the sake of the gospel.

Working with others takes a great deal of effort and is sometimes complicated, but we must enter into it for the cause of Christ. This is where missionary societies are often of great help, acting as facilitators and administrators in the task of mission.

We must establish self-supporting, missionary-minded churches.

The aim of missionary work is to plant churches, just as Paul did. Ultimately we want these to become self-supporting, and then contribute to the missionary cause as they follow the leading of the church's head, the Lord Jesus Christ.

We must lower our expectations from this life.

In the West we have swallowed too much the philosophy of the age that tells us to 'eat, drink and be merry, for tomorrow we die'. We need to be shaped by the 'economics' of Christ rather than consumer culture.

We must be joyously satisfied with Christ.

If we don't treasure the Lord Jesus Christ, we won't be willing to suffer for the sake of his name.

We must be convinced that the missionary task will be successful.

Nothing is going to thwart God's plans and purposes. The task of taking the gospel to all the nations of the earth is not beyond the church of Jesus Christ (Matthew 24:14). We must remember it is God's work and all we do is in dependence upon him. He will indeed build his church (16:18).

High profile

So how can we put these conclusions into practice in our local churches? Certainly, if we are going to take these principles and their implications seriously, missionary work must have a high profile in the life of the church.

It is not enough merely to pin up a few out-of-date missionary photographs on a world map or add to the piles of prayer letters at the back of the church building. Missionary work is at the heart of what God is doing in our world and we must make sure it has a central place in our church life. We need to be systematic and serious in our use of money. We must give time and energy to keeping up-to-date with those we support on the mission field and make sure their needs are brought regularly before the throne of grace. We should work together with other churches and societies.

The size of the task means that we cannot follow all missionary work to the same extent. We will, therefore, probably be involved at three different levels. First, we can have a general world interest. *Operation World* helps with this dimension, as does the regular Missionary Spotlight of *ET* and missionary reports in other Christian journals. It is now more possible to stay informed about what God is doing throughout the world than ever before.

Second, we can have a general interest in specific missions. Different churches will find they are naturally aligned with various missionary organisations due to theological agreement. These links mean the churches will follow their missionary endeavours in closer detail.

Third, churches can cultivate a specific interest in particular missionaries. We can be their prayer partners, becoming familiar with all the details of their day-to-day lives and work. We can 'adopt' such as 'our' missionaries and follow specific work in particular locations.

Practice and resources

Here are some intensely practical suggestions:

1. Why not have a weekly slot, say on a Sunday evening, that keeps worldwide missionary work in view? In just a few minutes a brief report can be given about a country, and the needs of that country remembered in prayer. This helps to make believers 'world Christians'.

2. Why not 'adopt' an unreached people-group in prayer and ask God to establish a church among them? This prayer interest can be added to by supporting those missionaries trying to reach that group. For example, we can support people translating the Scriptures. How exciting to be playing our part in taking the gospel to the unreached nations of the world!

3. Many churches find it beneficial to have one prayer meeting each month with a specific missionary focus, where missionary news is shared and specific needs are brought before our God.

4. There are other ways to give missionary work the attention it needs. In our church we found it helpful to have a fellowship tea every few months on a Sunday afternoon, with a brief mission focus and prayer time included. This

has helped enthuse whole families about missionary work.

5. With many demands upon our limited resources, we must give missionary work the financial priority it needs. Many churches find it helpful to give a percentage of their regular income, say ten per cent, to missionary work. But why be satisfied with only ten per cent? Why not try to increase the percentage over time as the Lord gives the increase.

6. Those responsible for a church's programme should make sure they invite people involved in mission to come and speak of their work as often as possible, and to integrate this dimension into several aspects of church life.

7. Each Christian should pray regularly that the Lord will thrust forth labourers from his or her own congregation so that they too will have the privilege of being a sending church into the mission field.

The Great Commission demands that we make every effort to be missionary-minded churches. It will require energy and organisation from church leaders and full commitment from church members, but for the sake of Christ's name it will all be immensely worthwhile.

CHAPTER 8

RECEIVING A DEPUTATION

For many church members, it will be visits from missionaries and their representatives that most impact their view of mission work. So what does Scripture teach about hosting a missionary deputation meeting?

At the end of Paul's first missionary journey, he and Barnabas returned to Antioch—the church that had commended them to the grace of God and sent them out to preach the gospel.

Luke describes this first missionary deputation meeting: 'Now when they had come and gathered the church together, they reported all that God had done with them, and that he had opened the door of faith to the Gentiles. So they stayed there a long time with the disciples' (Acts 14:27-28).

What excitement and joy must have filled the people's hearts as they gathered to hear all that God had been pleased to do!

Opportunity and opposition

They heard how Paul and Barnabas had travelled to Cyprus, preaching the gospel from Salamis to

Paphos. God was evidently with them and the proconsul, Sergius Paulus, had been soundly converted. Moving on to Asia Minor, they had preached in the synagogue in Pisidian Antioch—where at one stage 'almost the whole city came together to hear the word of God' (13:44).

This aroused much jealousy among the Jewish leaders and led to their expulsion from the region. By now a pattern of opportunity, conversion and opposition was beginning to emerge.

The church would have listened intently as Paul related how, at Iconium, 'a great multitude both of the Jews and of the Greeks believed' (14:1). But imagine the people's concern as they heard what had happened at Lystra. At first the missionaries had been hailed as gods, but later were dragged out of the city and stoned.

Nevertheless, despite such opposition, the advance of the gospel could not be halted. The listeners must have marvelled at the missionaries' courage as they subsequently revisited the cities where they had suffered persecution, 'strengthening the souls of the disciples' and 'exhorting them to continue in the faith' (14:22).

Rejoicing

Having heard such a report, the people must have returned to their homes encouraged and strengthened in their own faith—glad that Paul and Barnabas were safely back with them but also rejoicing that God had wonderfully opened a door of faith to the Gentiles.

They had received stirring confirmation that the gospel really is good news for all the nations of the world. God had done great things. He had clearly used his missionary servants and heard the prayers of the sending church. What an encouragement it must have been to hear these missionaries speak of their work.

Thankfully, we still have opportunities to hear about, and be involved in, the work of mission. Indeed, this account in Acts ought to stir up and inspire pastors and churches to make their own plans to receive missionaries on deputation.

The deputation meeting today

Acts 14 shows how important missionary deputation meetings are for the growth and expansion of the church worldwide. Paul and Barnabas' work was not complete until they had returned and reported back.

We, too, should see such meetings as a vital part of our church's involvement in Christ's Great Commission. Mission work ought to be a clear priority for every local church. We best express our concern for and involvement in world mission by welcoming and hearing those working on the field.

Acts 14 emphasises the *priority* the church gave to hearing from Paul and Barnabas about their missionary endeavours. The *whole* church gathered—not just a handful of committed people.

We are not told whether the meeting involved just one gathering or several. It might have been a day conference on the Lord's Day or some other occasion. But whenever it took place it was given a high priority in the life of the church.

The narrative even suggests that it may have taken precedence over the church's regular meetings. They really wanted to hear what God was doing through those they had sent out. We also need to ensure that missionaries are given the priority their work deserves when they visit us.

How long?

We are told that Paul and Barnabas spoke of *all* that God had done through them. I don't believe for one moment that they could have done that in a five-minute slot in the morning service! The church was eager to hear and learn.

Adequate time was given so that the people could grasp what had happened and learn how the gospel had broken through into the Gentile world in such an amazing way. God's promises and plans were being worked out before their eyes.

We need to ensure that when missionaries come to us they are given adequate time to convey what God is doing in other lands and cultures as he fulfils his saving purposes in Christ.

How does it work in practice?

Once we have grasped how important these meetings are, we need flexibility, creativity and commitment to maximise the opportunities we have. Missionary meetings do not just have to be on a Wednesday evening!

Sometimes it may be good to change the night of our midweek meeting or combine with another church to hear a missionary who is visiting the area. Missionaries on deputation often find it hard to fill Mondays, Fridays and Saturdays.

So why not have a breakfast meeting on a Saturday morning? What about a Friday or Saturday night missionary rally aimed at young people from churches in the area? How about a day conference with several missionaries or mission societies? The opportunities are limitless if only we put our minds to the matter and give it the priority it deserves.

If you are privileged to have a missionary visit on a Sunday, why restrict him or her to an after-church meeting in the evening when everybody is tired and full from the day's ministry? Why not have them speak in the afternoon or as part of the service?

Most of the men supported by EMF are preachers, and many can preach in English as well as speak about their work. Would it not do our people good to hear God's Word being expounded by those who normally work on the frontline of gospel missionary endeavour?

Those of us who are pastors and leaders of churches should seek to plan ahead to give such meetings a priority in church life. In doing so we shall ensure that our church is as well-informed as those in Antioch concerning the work of the gospel overseas.

CHAPTER 9
A CASE STUDY—
JOHN CALVIN'S
MISSION TO FRANCE

The year 2009 is the 500th anniversary of the birth of John Calvin. He was born in northern France and was converted, as a student, in the early 1530s. From 1541 until his death in 1564 he served as a preacher and teacher in Geneva.

Calvin was never interested in study or teaching just for its own sake. He recognised that all study of God's Word and all Bible teaching must be assessed by its usefulness, and that usefulness is seen in how it aids the spread of the gospel.

And yet it is often claimed that Calvin showed no inclination towards missionary effort. He has been accused of being completely blind to the church's responsibility for worldwide mission. However, this view of Calvin's work is a complete myth.

Missionary centre

Calvin was in fact the director of an international, underground evangelistic mission. Geneva became the major missionary sending centre of the time. Missionaries went to many parts of Europe, but there were two main fields of concern—France and Brazil. In this chapter we are concerned with the mission to France.

During Calvin's time, Geneva became a place of refuge for thousands of Christians fleeing Catholic persecution across Europe. The majority of them came from France, but they did not come only as asylum-seekers. They also came to learn. Calvin took the opportunity to teach and train them so that they could carry the gospel back to their homelands.

Calvin understood that a good missionary has to be a good theologian. So he gave daily Bible lectures to equip them for their future work. In 1559 the Geneva Academy was launched. Now, the training became more systematic.

The academy was specifically set up to train missionary pastors to plant churches throughout Europe, but it had a particular vision and burden for France.

By 1564 the academy had several hundred students. In addition to their studies at the academy, missionary candidates were given practical experience. Some served as preachers in village churches around Geneva; others worked as chaplains in the city or as tutors to well-to-do families.

Before a missionary candidate was allowed to leave for his assignment, he was interviewed by the elders of the Genevan church. They made sure that his theology was sound. They heard him preach and checked that he had mastered the biblical languages.

They also made sure that he was morally upright and of sufficiently robust constitution, for they knew the work of pioneering the gospel in unevangelised Europe would be arduous.

Danger

We cannot be sure exactly when the mission to France began. It was some time between 1553 and 1555. Each year a number of men were sent as missionaries from Geneva. The peak years of missionary activity were 1561 and 1562, because of political developments in France at that time.

The French churches had been suffering severe repression at the hands of the Catholic establishment. But for those two years the authorities became preoccupied with rivalry between competing government factions. As a result there was a brief lull in the persecution, and the Genevan church seized its window of opportunity.

The records of the Genevan church list 88 men by name who went as missionaries to France. However, it does not name every missionary. We know that in 1561 alone 142 missionaries left Geneva for France. The fact that only twelve of these men are named in the records suggests that many hundreds of missionaries must have been commissioned during the final ten years of Calvin's life.

Of the 88 missionaries whose names we know, 62 were French by birth. That means that the other

26 were cross-cultural missionaries in the fullest sense of the term.

The reason so few of the missionaries were identified by name has to do with security. The French church was facing fierce opposition from the Catholic establishment. The missionary operation had to be carried out secretly.

If they were too open about what they were doing, they would have been in danger. Some of the missionaries travelled under assumed names. They avoided roads, making their way by foot along mountain by-ways.

Missionary activity took the form of evangelism and church-planting. The missionaries would gather a group in a home. Members of the group would invite their friends and relatives.

Secret meetings

They would meet at night behind heavy curtains. If a home was not available, they would hold their meetings in barns, or even in the open air in some secluded spot, such as the middle of a wood. They identified escape routes and hiding places in case they were needed.

Calvin had himself experienced underground church life some years earlier. In 1535 he had fled from persecution in Paris and lived in Poitiers for a couple of years. While there, he conducted secret services in a cave outside the city and held secret evangelistic meetings in homes. No doubt, the memory of this period of his life served him well in planning the missionary venture twenty years later.

In spite of their carefulness, it was not always possible for the missionaries to avoid the attention of hostile parties. Often the authorities got wind of what was going on. Meetings were interrupted; congregations were dispersed. Several of the Genevan missionaries were caught and martyred; this applied to nine of the 88 whose names we know.

When sufficient people were converted, a church was constituted. In the four years from 1555 to 1559, nearly 100 churches were planted and constituted. By 1562, that number had risen to well over 2,000.

One interesting result of the mission was the conversion of many members of the French aristocracy, including some relatives of the French royal family.

It has been estimated that, by 1562, half the French nobility were Calvinistic Christians. This was a bonus, because it meant that Protestant congregations could meet in relative safety on the estates of Christian landowners.

Christian literature

Calvin believed that the ministry of literature was vital for the spread of the true gospel. He placed great emphasis on the printing of tracts, pamphlets, books and Bibles. In fact, printing became the major industry in sixteenth-century Geneva.

There were at least 34 printing presses operating by 1563. Large paper mills and ink-making factories were built. More paper was bought in from elsewhere. A high proportion of Geneva's population was employed in this industry—as printers, paper-manufacturers, ink-makers, editors, proof-readers and authors.

A commission on printing was set up. Its task was to make sure that everything published was doctrinally sound and to co-ordinate the work of the various printers and prevent unnecessary duplication. Nearly 40 publications appeared every year.

Calvin himself was very active in writing books against the errors of Catholicism. These works offered guidance to the young French church and made a large contribution to the success of the mission.

The southern French city of Lyon was a major trade centre. It was quite close to the Swiss border and to Geneva, the border city. Much literature was smuggled into France and then spread throughout the country via Lyon.

Calvin and his colleagues in Geneva clearly gave the missionary effort to France a remarkably high priority. Sometimes they were prepared to allow their own churches to go without pastors so that more men could go out as missionaries.

Missionary

One thing that stands out in this story is Calvin's

definition of a missionary. He used the term exclusively of a man who was an ordained preacher of the gospel, who planted churches and then pastored the flock. Essentially, a missionary was no different from any other full-time minister; it was merely that he was sent to a place further afield.

In recent times, the word 'missionary' has become so diluted that almost any activity can now be construed as Christian mission. It is certainly the case that there are many forms of service which are valid expressions of Christian calling. However, Calvin was wise to retain the notion of mission for frontline evangelism and church-planting.

Similarly, William Carey distinguished between missionaries who were men ordained to preach the gospel, and those necessary companions of missionaries who attended to other needs on the field. We would do well today to restore this biblical distinction and emphasis.